Flipping Houses for Beginners

How to Flip a House and Make a Profit

by Courtney Copeland

Table of Contents

Introduction

It is not easy to find a job or business venture that will guarantee financial success in today's trying economy. It is a discouraging fact that most salaried workers can barely stretch their earnings to last until the next payday, and small businesses crumble before generating a satisfactory ROI (Return on Investment).

Even so, with a bit of research and calculated risk-taking, there is great potential to earn good money from certain business ventures -- particularly, in flipping houses. With the right know-how, flipping houses can make around $60,000 to $120,000 *per flip*. This business is now starting to become a lucrative source of income as people have started buying houses again.

The process is relatively simple: You buy a house at cut-price, renovate and make improvements on it, and then sell it at a higher price within a period of 6 months. If you follow the guidelines in this book and make smart choices along the way, you'll be earning six figures in no time at all.

Although the process is simple, that doesn't make it easy. You have to know exactly what you will have to do before you go putting all your hard-earned money into a single property. What types of houses can you buy to maximize profits? Where will you look for these houses? Are there legal issues that you must settle before making a purchase? These are among the questions that you should be able to answer before beginning the process of flipping houses.

In this book, we will look at the answers to these questions and more. This book will review the house flipping process in detail and provide the steps you can take to flip successfully, and earn yourself a solid profit each time.

Chapter 1: Understanding House Flipping

Put simply, house flipping or flipping houses is making a business of buying a run-down house, renovating it, and then reselling it for a profit. Your foremost priority is deciding where to buy a house that will gain you the most profit. To know the answer to this question, spend some time to familiarize yourself with the various real estate listings in and around the area that you are interested in. If you haven't yet, you need to become intimately familiar with the online MLS system.

The best place to scout for these types of houses is in foreclosed-home sales. With a little diligence, you could also find some cheap houses from real estate listings. You should always be cautious, however, because your money may go down the drain if you choose a house that cannot sell at a higher price quickly after you've invested time and money to renovate it.

The Essential Requirements: What you need

1. **Up-to-date real estate information.**

   Reliable information about your target property and the community around it will help you arrive at sound decisions. Ensuring that the property is located at a strategic area near important institutions such as schools, hospitals, recreational places and malls is a prerequisite. The cost of the house is also something you must consider. Will you be able to resell it at a price high enough to recover whatever expenditures you incur, plus profit?

2. Sufficient cash

You'll need enough cash for the required down payment, and for the improvement, renovation or remodeling of the house. In addition, you may require cash for other miscellaneous expenses. The amount of cash that must be at your disposal will depend upon the cash value of the house you plan to buy.

3. Good credit standing

A good or excellent credit score will be handy in case there is a need for additional cash. On top of the house renovations, there are other expenses that you will have to shoulder and prepare for; there are also realtor's fees and other contingency expenses to consider.

4. Ready market

As you begin the process of flipping a house, it helps if you already have a certain "type" of prospective buyer in mind. For example, are the house, its amenities, and the neighborhood best suited for a young professional couple who might be starting a new family? Or for empty nesters looking to downsize after their kids went off to college? Or for a University professor who would be able to walk or ride a bike to the nearby campus? In any case, refrain from giving a house tour, however, until all renovation work is completed because the construction clutter will decrease the impact of your presentation. This will make it difficult to quote a good price to your buyer later on after the project is complete.

5. A team of experts

If you're new to flipping houses, you will learn that hiring professionals will be costly. In cases like this, you have the option to research on your own and do the homework that other experts would normally be called in for. If you can spare the time, you can enroll in affordable online courses and save on professional fees by being your own home inspector, appraiser, realtor, interior decorator, architect, or accountant. Doing some, or all, of these things for your house is a cost-saving measure.

6. An entrepreneur's persona

Excellent house flippers tend to possess these three specific personality traits: patience, diligence and flexibility. Flipping houses requires hard work, especially during the first few transactions. You have to be patient and diligent in doing research in order to avoid losing money, and more importantly, increase profits. Also, you'll need to be flexible in so far as having an ability to change your "game plan" during the purchase or sales phases if need be, since it's not unusual for real estate transactions to go not-as-planned.

With these basic requirements covered, you will be well on your way to start your house flipping business.

Chapter 2: How to Flip a House and Make a Profit

To ensure that you make a nice profit from flipping houses, there are specific steps you must take. Let the steps below guide you in creating a low-risk action plan and start making a profit through flipping houses:

Step #1 – Prepare a Plan of Action (POA)

A business plan or plan of action (POA) serves as a blueprint of the things you intend to accomplish. This is an important first step because this will help keep your business on the right track. It allows you to organize your resources, anticipate problem areas and evaluate the best course of action.

A complete business plan includes a timetable that should schedule the sale of the renovated house to be completed within a 6 month period. The specific budget for the different steps must also be included in your POA. The details of your expected outputs and results should be written down as well. A meticulously prepared business plan saves precious time and money. Banks, moneylenders, investors and business partners will also want to review this document when you start to make arrangements for financing.

Step #2 - Explore the market

Research diligently for a house located at a strategic area that you can buy at a low price. Foreclosed houses are typically a good choice for houses to flip. You should also be on the look-out for properties that are marked "rush sale" as owners in a hurry to sell are sometimes willing to accept less than market value. There are good houses that are sold in the market due to emergency situations, such as transfers of residence or divorces. Be aware, though, that the market varies by state, so take time to do research before signing purchase agreements. Learn the rules and methods of flipping houses that will apply to your target location as these can differ in every state.

Double check the following:

> **Cost of the property** – How much does the property cost? Can you possibly get a superb ROI from it? This is where your skills as an evaluator will come in handy. As a flipper, you have to be very hands-on throughout the entire process.

➢ **Condition of the house** – Is the foundation strong and well-planned? Are the walls of the house still sturdy? Will you need to do a complete renovation, or does the property need minor repairs only? Make cost estimates and study potential sale prices before making a purchase because you might spend a great deal, and wind up getting nothing in return.

➢ **Location of the property** – As mentioned earlier, the location of the property is critical to your success. Is the property located in an area where it can be sold quickly? It ought to be within the vicinity of major service centers and institutions. Being a stone's throw away from the center of commerce and education will reduce the cost of travel. This is an advantageous selling point that you can mention to prospective buyers.

➢ **Condition of the surrounding neighborhood** – Is the property in a safe community? What is the crime rate? Are the other rental houses around occupied all year round? Do majority of the people stay until old age? If there are several empty houses and no one is willing to stay long, then it is a sign that you should focus your sights elsewhere. The house may be low-priced, but you will likely have difficulty selling it later on. If it isn't sold quickly, you will spend more money with the maintenance of the house.

➢ **Add-ons** – Are there good add-ons, such as: durable carpets, useful built-in closets, and extra amenities (fireplace, game tables or music rooms)? Take note of these add-ons as they give extra value to the house.

Step #3 – Narrow your choices and inspect them personally

After exploring all the options available, the next thing to do is pick your top choices. It's best to tour your top two or three houses physically, rather than doing so online. There may be areas or aspects that cannot be viewed on a virtual tour.

It's better to be cautious and nitpick to ensure that you're buying a house that needs as little renovation as possible. Keep a notebook with you so you can write down the pros and cons of each of your choices. This will allow you to review the entries later on. Never buy a property that you have not personally visited. The time invested in viewing the unit is always worth it.

Step #4 - Estimate the cost of renovations

Once you've got your eyes set on a house, you need a competent estimator at the onset of your flipping business, unless you're a qualified estimator yourself. The estimator will compute the projected cost of the entire project, including the processing of legal documents, the renovation, and the estimated timeframe it will take to sell the house.

If you find the costs acceptable and are ready to purchase, proceed to step #5. If not, you can take advantage of a mortgage, or other funding sources as outlined in Chapter 4. Search for those that offer low interests. You don't want to be up to your neck in debt before you have even succeeded in your first house flipping venture.

Step #5 – Negotiate to buy the property

Buy the house at the lowest price you can negotiate. It is important to note that the cheapest price may not always be the best, especially if you have to perform major renovations that will put a sizeable hole in your wallet. Be a smart flipper by adding together the total purchase costs of the house and the estimated cost of its renovation. The numbers will help you arrive at a final decision about purchasing the property. This will ensure that the money you give upfront is worth the property you're buying.

Make use of your good credit record, should you need additional funding. Also, be sure that you have verified and received your copies of all the pertinent legal documents.

Step #6 – Obtain your renovation/building permit from designated institutions

Before you begin with the renovations or remodeling, you must first secure the necessary construction permits. Neglecting to acquire and display your building permit can be costly. Minor repairs such as replacing a patio or adding built-in cabinets normally don't require permits. However, for major repairs such as room additions, alterations and kitchen remodeling, you will need a building permit. The designated authorities in your state can provide you with the guidelines in securing a permit. Inquire from the City Mayor's Office or another local agency.

Step #7 - Renovate the house

You should plan to renovate the house as quickly as possible, so you can get your money back with a tidy profit. As mentioned, the ideal timeframe is within 6 months. Delaying the re-sale of the house any further will be a disadvantage to you, because you'll be spending more for its maintenance the longer you keep it. The important thing is to renovate or remodel all damaged areas of the house to ensure that you'll get the best reselling price. Fixing minor damage yourself can help cut costs. But for dangerous repairs such as electric wiring, you will have to hire an expert.

Attend to the worst damaged areas first to ensure that they're not overlooked. Decide wisely when to enlist the help of contractors. Save money by actively participating in the renovation. To start with, you can do some cleaning and discard old items yourself. Remember to prepare another time table in which to accomplish this particular step, and stick to it. The faster you are able to flip houses, the faster you can generate more income.

Rooms and Spaces that require special attention

➤ **The entrance to the house** – The entrance to the house should be outstanding, in order to immediately capture the buyer's interest. Otherwise, you can lose a potential buyer with a sloppy and unwelcoming gate or entrance. Include the landscape of the front yard to add a welcoming atmosphere for any season of the year. You'll have to add finishing touches that reflect the present season to enhance the ambiance. When it's winter, warm, bright interior curtains can enliven the mood. During summer, use light willowy curtains to add a cheerful touch.

Keep the garden well-manicured, the pathway sparkling clean, and the entry doorway clutter-free and enticing. Use your imagination to motivate the buyers to enter the house. That's why it's crucial to know a little bit about your buyer's preferences. If possible, do some research about your prospective buyers. Flipping houses requires some skills in the sales department, too.

➤ **The yard** – Remember to devote some love and care to this area, because it will be the front runner when you present the house to a prospective buyer.

➢ **The kitchen** – You prepare your food in the kitchen. Therefore, it should always be spotlessly clean. Although you may not be changing the tiles of the sink, you will have to clean it until it looks brand-new. Wooden boards should be discarded and replaced if they ruin the appearance of the kitchen.

➢ **De-clutter all rooms** – Make sure that the pile of newspapers in the living room is discarded, and that the windowsills are free of dirt and dust. Empty the bathroom closet and drawers of everything. Your potential buyer isn't interested in the brand of shaving cream that you're using. Remove all personal items lying around the house. It has to appear to be a brand-new house. For these minor tasks, you can hire people to work for you on a part time or contractual basis.

➢ **Create a clean and fresh ambiance** – Would you buy a house that stinks as soon as you set foot on its entrance? Probably not. This is a sure turn-off for most buyers. Allow proper ventilation, so that unpleasant odors won't sabotage your efforts to flip the house quickly. Use mild air fresheners to eliminate stubborn odors. Check all corners of the house, including the back and front yard, to ensure that odors do not come from uncollected garbage or hidden rotting materials.

➤ **Pay attention to the small details** – Renovate the house as though you yourself will be living in it. Repair even the small fixtures, change all dirty light bulbs. Keep the windows and corners dust free. Wash the muddy walkway and clean out the water in the garden pond. Don't think the buyer will ignore these little things. You can never assume in these instances. A little mistake can prove costly.

➤ **Opt for durable and competitive prices when buying renovation materials** – The cost of a given material doesn't always indicate durability. There are inexpensive materials that are just as durable as their pricey counterparts. Stretch the value of your dollar by patiently searching and asking experts. There is no shortage of information about great building materials online if you only look.

Step #8 – Relist the newly-renovated house

The end of your renovation signifies that you are now ready to sell or relist the house. One way is to enlist your property with legitimate realtors. Another way is to sell your house directly to a prospective buyer. This would depend on how broad your network is. Is your marketing network able to reach a large number of potential buyers? The next step gives suggestions on how to ask for help from your social media connections as well.

It is also time to compute the list price for the house. Set a price that will leave you a good profit after you have paid all the expenditures (major and minor) that you have incurred in buying and renovating the house. Don't forget to add your advertising fees to your expenses. Compare your price with those houses already existing in the area with the same specifications. Offer competitive prices to attract potential buyers.

Step #9 – Advertise in every possible venue

Aside from enlisting the house with real estate brokers, you can also go online and notify your social media community. Facebook, Twitter, Instagram, and the like can significantly help get the word out. House flipping has a much better chance of succeeding when pertinent details are posted on your website or blog. You can set it so that site visitors can view photos and even go on a virtual video tour of the property. Submitting the house details to Craiglist and similar sites can also help increase your chances of a sale.

Advertising in local newspapers, radio stations and TV are additional options you can consider. The least expensive method is online advertising because you can always display your ads on your user profiles in social media and social bookmarking sites for free. Of course, you can opt for paid advertisements on these and other sites if you have allotted a budget for this type of advertising.

On the other hand, you can stage the house. This is another effective selling strategy that can facilitate sales. Present the elegance, comfort and superb ambiance of the different rooms of the house to win over potential buyers.

Step #10 – Present the house to your prospective buyer

A house tour allows you to showcase the advantages your prospective buyer stands to gain from buying the house. But, be careful that you don't mislead the buyer. Disclose all known issues about the house. Informing him about the necessity to upgrade the house's plumbing every year will make him realize everything is upfront with you.

Transparency will earn the trust of your buyer and will eventually help you conclude the sale. Your name as a reputable house flipper will help you earn significantly more in the long run. If you treat them honestly and sincerely, they'll readily endorse you to their family members and friends. Word-of-mouth is still the most reliable advertisement method around, even with the rise of social media.

If you are using a real estate agent to help you list the house who will be walking the prospective buyers through your house, then do a few practice walkthroughs with your agent so that you can point out the highlights that you want to be sure he mentions to the buyers. You can even pretend that you are the agent, and that the agent is the prospective buyer.

Step #11 – Conclude the sale as soon as possible

Do what you can to finalize the sale ASAP. Be prepared to close the deal promptly to lessen your expenditures. For a house flipper, every day wasted is money lost. So be ready with the necessary documents such as the notarized "Deed of Sale" and other official receipts. As the seller, it is also your responsibility to settle any tax liability and liens. Once the property goes into your buyer's hands, you surrender all your rights and responsibilities to the property.

Congratulate yourself at this point, for you have successfully flipped a house! Now, you're ready to start the process of flipping another house anew. You may have even been scouting the MLS and foreclosure listings while your other house was for sale. If so, you're a step ahead, which is a sign of a successful flipper.

Chapter 3: Where to Find Suitable Houses to Flip

One of the initial challenges to flipping houses is where to look for suitable houses. The foremost is to choose from foreclosed houses or go through the MLS online or as provided to you by local real estate agents. However, there are other lesser-known sources that you can also look into. This is a list that can assist you in finding suitable houses to flip.

1. **Probate house sales**

    These probate sales are good sources of houses to flip because they properties are offered at affordable, discounted prices. Sometimes the people concerned would like to see their inherited properties converted into cash as soon as possible, and that's where you can come in.

2. **Online listings of individual sellers**

    There are online users who are in dire need of money and are selling their houses as direct sellers to whoever may be interested. This transaction will eliminate the fees for real estate brokers, which is an advantage for you. This listing may be posted on the person's blog, website or social sites of which he or she is a member.

3. Property Wholesalers

Wholesalers of houses are great sources of houses to flip. They can also offer cheaper prices for the houses overall. All you need to do is to find out who the wholesalers are within your area.

4. Multiple Listing Service (MLS)

As I mentioned before, you should be searching the house listings of MLS available online, which consists of all houses that are for sale. There are many different MLS websites. Some of my favorites include ZipRealty.com and TheMLS.com. You can do an advance search to specify the price ranges you can afford and the number of rooms or the other details that you want. From the results you can select the best house to flip. During the initial stages of step one, where you create your business plan, it is helpful to do a bit of research with MLS house listings to get an idea of the costs and estimates of property in a specific area.

5. **Auctions of on-hold properties because of tax problems**

These are houses that have been put on hold due to tax issues. The local sheriff will usually have information about these house auctions. Oftentimes they go up for sale at an auction at a specific time of year, then after you've won the auction, the taxpayer still has a certain amount of time to pay their past due taxes. If they do, you don't get the house. If they don't, then they get kicked out and the property is all yours. The process varies in different municipalities, so be sure to check with your county official, as it may work differently there.

6. **Other online listings**

There are also other websites that can connect you to a property seller. This can be more expensive though because the middle man, which is the website, typically charges fees. Examples of these websites are: Zillow.com and Homes.com. A quick online search will show you a string of websites offering to connect you with sellers located in your own state.

7. Local newspaper

The leading local newspaper will surely have a list of houses on sale in your location. Choose from this list and do an ocular visit to determine the house's suitability for flipping.

8. Television

Television is a good source of houses for sale. Just be ready with your pen and paper to list down telephone numbers and addresses.

9. Radio

For those who cannot afford the expensive prices of written and TV ads, the radio is a splendid choice. It can reach your local community and you can easily conclude business with the house owners.

The important thing to remember when sourcing property is not to rush. Take the time to explore and inspect all the houses within your range and evaluate with the help of a reliable estimator.

Chapter 4: Financing your House Flipping Venture

One does not necessarily need to have a big capital in order to start a business. With a little research and preparation, you can find ways and means to raise funding for a new venture. The meticulous effort you put into creating your business plan will now bear fruit as you present the plan to people who can help fund your house flipping business. Listed below are the possible financing sources you can consider:

1. Business partners

A business partner, who will provide funding while you do the legwork and the flipping tasks, is a viable option. Both you and your partner can earn from your investments. He or she invests money, and you invest your time and effort. Create proper legal contracts to document every detail of your agreement and partnership to prevent potential legal issues later on.

2. Banks or lending companies

You can take out a bank loan as starting capital for your house flipping business. You have to earn more than what the bank demands as interest for your loan.

Opt for money-lenders who give you the lowest interest rating and those with flexible payment options.

3. Investors

Search for willing investors for your business. Your first investors may be your friends or family members, who trust you enough to invest. Gradually, as your business progresses, more and more investors will come to your assistance. Your good integrity as a house flipper will surely increase the number of your investors.

4. Personal savings

Another way to raise business capital is to save for it. You can use existing savings but be aware of the risks that are involved in doing so. We've heard it said: Don't dive into the water if you're uncertain of your success. Research and study all the aspects of the venture before plunging head on.

5. Government grants or loans

Inquire from your local or state government if there are grants and loans for small entrepreneurs or business owners like you. Prepare your Business Plan and Business Proposal for presentation. These plans have to outline clearly what you intend to do and achieve in your flipping business. Calculate how much interest you'll pay and compare it with your projected income from flipping a house. Government grants typically charge smaller interest rates than banks and lending companies so we recommend choosing this option if a grant is available.

6. Second mortgages

You can only avail of this type of funding if you don't have any options left. Before doing this, determine the equity of your home. If the equity is almost negative, look for other options of obtaining money. Since you're using a second mortgage, most likely, your house will serve as the collateral. Hence, when something goes wrong with your flipping business, you lose your house. Becoming homeless is not your goal. Use a second mortgage only when you're certain you can cover the scheduled payments. Nevertheless, risking big things to obtain bigger things is sometimes necessary in order to succeed. Go for it if you deem the risk is worth it.

7. Raise money

As a house flipper, you have to learn how to raise money for your next flip. Showing people how much they can earn as potential investors by helping you raise money is the general idea. Don't ask for money.

Let them voluntarily contribute their cash for your goal. Don't promise big earnings however. Explain to them comprehensively how flipping houses works so they can understand that their earnings is dependent on how successful your house flip is. They can act as secondary or primary investors with percentage earnings depending on the amount they invest.

8. Sellers

You can partner with a seller to flip a house, and then later on share in the proceeds of the business. He can also choose to be a silent partner and invest funds only, if he doesn't want any of the action.

9. Buyers

The same principle applies to your potential buyers of the renovated house; they can serve as partners or investors.

All of your agreements should have documents or contracts duly prepared by a licensed attorney to legalize the agreement. The details must be clearly stated and witnessed. Having a lawyer attend to the legal nitty-gritty will ensure that everything is done in accordance with the law.

Chapter 5: Final Pointers on Flipping Houses

Flipping houses can provide you a tidy profit if you take the time to learn the appropriate steps to become a successful house flipper. The previous chapters have emphasized the need for thorough market research and a hands-on approach. These finals tips should help further ease your venture:

1. **Don't overprice.** Your price should be competitive with other properties in that area. Compare your prices with that of other similar properties. Your price has to be reasonable - but not excessive.

2. **Accomplish all necessary paperwork timely and completely.** Each and every transaction should be properly documented to avoid unwanted legal issues.

3. **Become a student of home improvement.** Since your business is flipping houses, you will have to learn about home improvement, architecture and design. Grab this opportunity to acquire a new, useful skill.

4. **Understand the risks involved.** Know that there is an element of danger when it comes to flipping houses. When you go into the business without a clear picture of the risks, you can lose big money. Lessen your risks by being conservative with your estimations. Get a second appraisal of the cost of buying and renovating the house to ensure your figures are correct. Also, researching intensively about the area where you'll buy the house is crucial.

5. **Sell at the right time.** Selling at the right time can dictate the success or failure of your house flipping. For example, listing a ranch house during the winter months will probably attract less prospective buyers. However, you can counter this by designing the house to accommodate the season, like prepping the house to look like a winter retreat. Or, during the summer, by adding a flower garden to the front yard. Small touches like this will surely attract more buyers.

6. **Get the help of a competent estimator after renovations.** You have to know the correct estimation of the value of the house. You can't just name a list price without computing and comparing against the existing prices of houses of the same size and make.

7. **Consider hiring an attorney.** This is vital if you plan to extend the network of your flipping business. The upfront cost of acquiring a lawyer may be costly, but is definitely cheaper and preferable to facing legal battles. When your business booms, you'll need a competent attorney to oversee the legal aspects of your business.

8. **Form a team of experts or subcontractors.** If you plan to stay in this business, you'll have to hire your own team of experts. This will shorten your turn around time and bring in more sales. Make sure though that you keep track of the added costs and price accordingly.

As with most worthwhile endeavors, one must remain flexible and be ready to modify these tips based on your specific situation. As long as you remain level headed, you will be able to overcome and come out on top.

Conclusion

Flipping houses is a business venture worth seriously considering. It's a huge money earner if you act timely and follow the formula already tried and tested successfully by so many others. Take note that your primary goal is to earn a profit by buying a house at a cut-rate price and later selling it at a premium, after having added value by renovating and remodeling.

If you choose to go into this lucrative business, be aware of the risks that you may encounter. Don't be discouraged easily though, because starting any business involves some risks. With careful planning and a bit of courage, you will be able to surpass the challenges that the business may bring.

With the information in this book, we are confident you can increase your chances of success. Keep this as a handy reference as you take the plunge and become a highly efficient house flipper.

Last, I'd like to thank you for purchasing this book! If you enjoyed it or found it helpful, I'd greatly appreciate it if you'd take a moment to leave a review on Amazon. Thank you!

36215668R00029

Made in the USA
Middletown, DE
26 October 2016